Daniel Boone

Frontier Hero

To Bob, our friend and builder,
who faces every challenge with the adventurous
spirit of our frontier ancestors.

— *E.R. & D.B.*

ISBN 0-590-47901-6

Copyright © 1996 by Don Bolognese and Elaine Raphael.
All rights reserved. Published by Scholastic Inc.
CARTWHEEL BOOKS and the CARTWHEEL BOOKS logo
are registered trademarks of Scholastic Inc.

12 11 10 9 8 7 6 5 4 3 2 1   1   7 8 9/9 0 1 2/0

Daniel Boone

Frontier Hero

by Elaine Raphael and Don Bolognese

Scholastic Inc.

New York   Toronto   London   Auckland   Sydney

The Summer Pasture

Sarah Boone called to her son as
she was preparing the noon meal,
"Daniel, is that a wolf I hear?"
Daniel stopped chopping wood and listened.
The wolf howled again.
Its cry echoed from a distant hill.
Daniel carried firewood into the cabin.

"The wolf is far away, Mother,
but to be safe I'll sleep by the cow pen."
"Thee is a good son, Daniel," said his mother,
and she handed him a steaming bowl of rabbit stew.

Later, Daniel walked the surrounding woods.
He searched for any sign of the wolf.
Daniel had no fear of the woods.
He liked being there alone.

The Panther

As Daniel grew older
he spent more time in the hills
of eastern Pennsylvania.
Sometimes he went hunting with Lone Eagle,
a friend from a nearby village.
One day, they came across signs of a bear.
Lone Eagle showed Daniel how to pick up its trail.
They followed its tracks, moving silently
through the woods.
Suddenly, Lone Eagle stopped.
Daniel stopped, too.
The two boys stood still and listened.

They heard a low growl.
Slowly Daniel looked up.
Ahead of them, on a branch, was a panther.
Lone Eagle looked at Daniel—and at his rifle.
Daniel knew that Lone Eagle trusted his skill.
If the panther charged, he would shoot.
The boys waited.
Then as quickly as it had come,
the panther was gone.
The two friends turned and left
as silently as the panther.

The Young Guide

A year later, early in May of 1750, a column
of Conestoga wagons waited in the rain.
Squire Boone, head of the large Boone clan,
stood alongside his son.
"Dan'l, if this rain keeps up, the trail
will turn into a river of mud."

"Don't worry, Pa," Daniel answered.
"I've hunted these mountains for two years.
I know every good trail and mountain pass
from here to the frontier."
Squire Boone looked up at his 15-year-old son.
Yes, he thought, *I've made a good choice.*
"Dan'l," he said, "if anyone can guide our family
to North Carolina, you can."
Daniel stood in his saddle and waved to the lead wagon.
Slowly, the column began to move.

Homestead

At the age of 21, Daniel married Rebecca Bryant.
All the neighbors came to help them
build their first house.
Daniel had promised Rebecca
that she'd have a home
and a fire in the hearth before the first snow.

Daniel stood on a half-finished wall,
waiting for the next log to be rolled up.
A hawk circled above him.
He watched as it hunted high above the woods.

A cold wind blew leaves from the nearby trees.
"Daniel," called his brother, Samuel.
Daniel kept staring at the woods.
He longed to be there.
"Daniel," his brother called again.
"We need more logs."
Daniel jumped down and picked up his ax.
"Winter's coming, Daniel," his brother said.
"I know, Samuel," Daniel answered excitedly,
"and as soon as this house is up,
I'm going hunting."

Rebecca Boone

It was still dark when Rebecca
hung the pot of porridge over the glowing ashes.
Her three children would wake to a hearty breakfast.
Rebecca's day was filled with many chores.
And now that Daniel was going on one of his
hunting trips, she would have even more.
Besides her housework and the children's lessons,
she had to run the farm, too.
Daniel loaded his packhorse with blankets,
sacks of dried corn, and salt.

"This time, Rebecca, I'm going to follow
the Warrior's Path to a place called Kanta-Ke.
Last trip, I almost got lost looking for it."
"I don't believe you could get lost
in the wilderness, Dan'l," Rebecca teased.
"I'll always find my way back to you, Rebecca,"
he answered.
Rebecca smiled but said nothing.
They kissed good-bye.
As Daniel disappeared into the woods,
Rebecca had a terrible fear
that she would never see him again.

The Warning

A year later Daniel was still hunting in Kentucky.
He had almost enough furs and hides to go home.
One evening, he returned to his camp
to find it surrounded by Indians.
Their leader was angry when he spoke.
"This is our hunting ground.
Those skins and furs belong to us."
He told his men to take all of Daniel's furs.

"Leave him a gun and moccasins."
The warrior glared at Daniel.
"Go back. Tell your people to stay away.
If you are so foolish to come here again,
the wasps and yellow jackets will sting you."
But Daniel did not leave.
He hid from the Indians and hunted.
He knew that some time soon,
he would bring his family to Kentucky.

The Wild Man

Planting time was over and everyone celebrated.
Rebecca was dancing with her daughter Levina
when suddenly her daughter cried out,
"Mama, Mama, look! A wild man."
Rebecca turned. She stared at the stranger.
He reached out for her, but she backed away.
"You need not refuse," said the stranger,
"for you have danced many a time with me."
When Rebecca heard his voice,
she threw her arms around him and began to cry.

It was Daniel—alive and home after two long years!
His neighbors gathered 'round to hear his story.
"Where've you been, Dan'l?" someone called out.
"In the richest land I've ever seen," he answered.
"Deep woods for hunting, good soil for growing corn,
meadows for grazing cattle and horses."
"Take us there, Dan'l!" another neighbor shouted.
"Someday," Daniel answered. "Someday we'll
all go to Caintuck together."

The Cumberland Gap

In the spring of 1775, Daniel and a group
of his neighbors set out for Kentucky.
Their job was to clear the trail for others
to follow.
Daniel and his daughter looked out
over miles of wooded hills.
"There it is, Susy — Caintuck —
just beyond the Cumberland Gap."
"Pa, it's beautiful."
Daniel nodded.
He hoped there was enough land
for his people and the Indians to share.

He remembered Chief Oconostota's words
when the deed was signed.
"Brother," the Cherokee Indian had said,
"we have given you a fine land,
but I believe you will have
much trouble in settling it."
Daniel understood.
He knew that life in Kentucky
would not be easy or safe.

In the summer of 1775, the settlers
built a fort on the banks of the Kentucky River.
They called it Boonesborough.

The Canoe Ride

A year later on a hot July day, Jemima Boone
and her friends, Betsy and Fanny,
took a canoe out on the river.
"My pa told me to stay close by," warned Jemima.
"Indians may be watching from the other shore."
"Oh, don't be a sissy," teased Betsy.
"We'll be safe in the middle."

They paddled off laughing and singing.
They didn't notice the strong current
carrying them toward the opposite shore.
Suddenly, someone grabbed the canoe.
The girls screamed.
Hands reached into the canoe
and dragged them onto the shore.
In minutes, the girls and their kidnappers
had disappeared into the forest.

The Chase

"They've taken the girls!"
The shouts were heard all through Boonesborough.
Daniel ran to the riverbank.
He sent men up and down the river.
"Find their trail!" he ordered.
"We must overtake them before
they reach their village."

The Indians hurried the frightened girls
through the woods.
Jemima knew her father would follow them.
She left signs — torn bits of her dress,
strands of hair, bent twigs.

When Fanny and Betsy cried, Jemima whispered,
"We must be brave; I'm sure my pa is on our trail."

By the third day Daniel and his men
caught up to the kidnappers.
Daniel looked down at them from a ridge.
He turned to his men and
gave a sign for complete silence.
The time had come to free the girls.

The Hero of Boonesborough

Rebecca Boone watched and waited
on the riverbank. Three days had passed,
and still no word about the girls.
Suddenly there was a call from the woods.
Rebecca froze—her heart seemed to stop.
A second later, she heard Daniel's voice.
"We have them. They're safe."
Crying and laughing, Rebecca ran to her daughter.

All of Boonesborough rushed
to greet the girls and their rescuers.
There were tears and hugs from everyone.
Then, one of Boone's men spoke up,
"Daniel, no one but you could have led us
through that wilderness."
Everyone began to cheer,
and the cheers echoed back and forth
across the hills of Kentucky.

Drawing America

You can draw Daniel Boone, his family, and the Indians of the Kentucky frontier. The following pages have pictures for you to copy and color. Copy the drawings freehand—or use our guidelines. Here's how:

1. Copy the blue guidelines first. Use an ordinary pencil and ruler.

2. After doing the guidelines, draw the main outlines one box at a time.

3. Finish the figure. Add details. Take your time. Copy one box at a time.

A frontier woman like Rebecca Boone had to carry water to her cabin from a spring or stream. She used buckets made from hollowed-out logs. Her clothes were simple and homemade. Her shoes (which she only wore in the winter) were moccasins with hard leather soles.

4. Erase your pencil guidelines before you start to color the drawing. Here's an idea. Enlarge your pencil drawing on a copy machine. Then color the large copy.

Watercolors and colored pencils were used to color these pictures. The same technique was used to do the illustrations for the story of Daniel Boone.

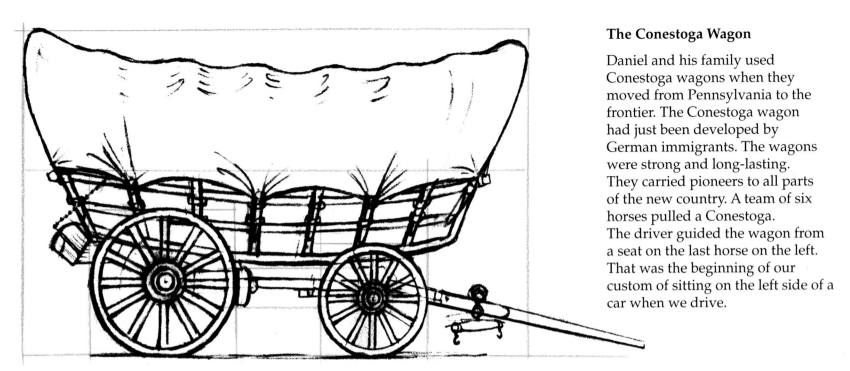

The Conestoga Wagon

Daniel and his family used Conestoga wagons when they moved from Pennsylvania to the frontier. The Conestoga wagon had just been developed by German immigrants. The wagons were strong and long-lasting. They carried pioneers to all parts of the new country. A team of six horses pulled a Conestoga.

The driver guided the wagon from a seat on the last horse on the left. That was the beginning of our custom of sitting on the left side of a car when we drive.

The Log Cabin

For the pioneer family, a log cabin was the perfect home. Wood was plentiful on the frontier, and with the help of neighbors, a 20-foot-by-16-foot log cabin could be built in four days.

The floor was packed earth. There were no windows. Light and heat came from a big fireplace. The log chimney was plastered with mud to keep it from burning.

Today it would be fun to go camping in a log cabin. To the frontier family of 1750, a log cabin was their only protection from the weather and the wilderness.

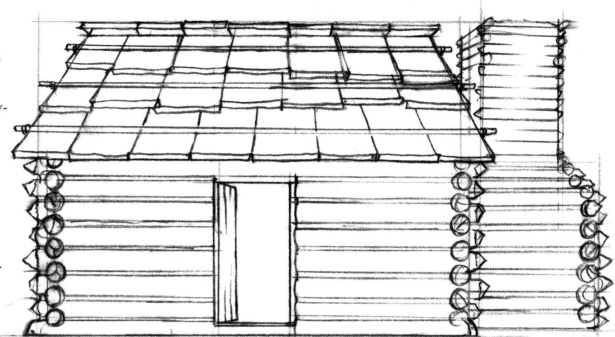

Shawnee, Cherokee, and Delaware Indians were some of the nations that lived and hunted along the Kentucky frontier.

This warrior is dressed in a style common to the Woodland tribes of that time. His sword was probably captured from a British soldier in the French-Indian War of 1755.

When Jemima Boone and her friends were captured, they were wearing their "Sunday best" clothes. During the kidnapping they were made to change their wooden-heeled shoes for moccasins.

The Indian-made bark canoe was a valuable means of travel in frontier days. The Indians and settlers also used the dugout, a boat made from a hollowed-out log.

A Note from the Authors

Daniel Boone had a long life with many more adventures. During the American Revolution, he saved Boonesborough from capture by the British. He explored more of the frontier, which led to more settlers moving west. He, too, moved west to Missouri with his family.

In his last years, he lived with his daughter Jemima. When Jemima was kidnapped she promised herself that if she ever saw her father again, she would never disobey him or be far away from him. True to her promise, she cared for her father until his death in 1820.